12.89

EXTREME MACHINES
ON WATER

PATRICIA ARMENTROUT

The Rourke Press, Inc.
Vero Beach, Florida 32964

Patricia Armentrout specializes in nonfiction writing and has had several
book series published for primary schools. She resides in Cincinnati with
her husband and two children.

PHOTO CREDITS:
© Paul Kemiel: cover; © Robert Brown/Intl. Stock: page 22; © Corel
Corporation: pages 4, 13, 15; © Defense Visual Information Center: pages
9, 18, 19; © Chad Ehlers/Intl. Stock: page 16; © Greg Johnston/Intl. Stock:
page 21; © Kadir Kir/Intl. Stock: page 12; © Peter Langone/Intl. Stock:
page 6; © Wilson North/Intl. Stock: page 7; © Panther Airboat: page 10

EDITORIAL SERVICES:
Penworthy Learning Systems

Library of Congress Cataloging-in-Publication Data

Armentrout, Patricia, 1960-
   Extreme machines on water / Patricia Armentrout.
      p. cm. — (Extreme machines)
   Includes index.
   Summary: Describes various water vehicles and their uses, including an aircraft
carrier, hydrofoil, and airboat.
   ISBN 1-57103-212-6
   1. Motorboats—Juvenile literature. 2. Ships—Juvenile literature. [1. Ships.]
I. Armentrout, Patricia. 1960- II. Title III. Series: Extreme machines.
VM150.A75 1998
623.8—dc21   98–20295
                                               CIP
                                             AC

Printed in the USA

TABLE OF CONTENTS

WHAT IS AN EXTREME MACHINE?

Since the invention of the first machine, people have worked to make machines bigger, faster, and better.

People use machines every day. Some machines make work easier. Some machines help us get from one place to another. Some machines are just for fun.

An **extreme** (ik STREEM) machine can be big or fast or just unusual.

A passenger hydrofoil starts to pick up speed.

AIRCRAFT CARRIER

The biggest warships are really floating airports. They are called aircraft carriers. The biggest are operated by the U.S. Navy.

Modern aircraft carriers, such as the USS Nimitz, are **nuclear-powered** (NOO klee ur POW erd).

The deck of an aircraft carrier is painted like an airport runway.

Navy aircraft line the deck of the USS Midway.

The nuclear reactors can power the Nimitz for 13 years before having to refuel.

The Nimitz, which is 1,092 feet (332 meters) long, has a crew of 6,000 and carries up to 90 aircraft. The aircraft take off from and land on the flight deck. Aircraft carriers may be the biggest extreme machine of them all.

HYDROFOIL

A **hydrofoil** (HY druh FOYL) is a very unusual boat. At slow speeds, a hydrofoil floats on water like most boats. As a hydrofoil picks up speed, it begins to lift out of the water. At high speeds most of the boat rides above the water.

A hydrofoil gets its lift from fins that remain underwater. Because the hydrofoil has less contact with the water, it is able to go much faster than ordinary boats.

A cruising Navy hydrofoil.

AIRBOAT

People who hunt and fish in swampy areas often prefer to travel on airboats. Airboats can skim across shallow water without getting stuck.

An airboat has a large fan, or prop, mounted at the rear of the boat. The fan sits above the water's surface inside a steel cage. The fan pushes the boat through the water.

If you get a chance to ride on an airboat, take along a good set of earplugs. Airboats are very noisy.

Airboats can move across shallow water without getting stuck.

POWERBOAT RACING

Powerboat racing is a thrilling sport. Drivers race crafts of all sizes—from small watercraft, like jet skis and wave runners, to big watercraft, like off-shore racers over 50 feet (15.25 meters) long.

Races are held on lakes, rivers, and oceans. A racecourse may be straight or have twists and turns.

Powerboats are built to handle high speeds.

An off-shore racer churns up the water on its way to victory.

The course is marked off with floating **buoys** (BOO eez).

The fastest powerboats can go over 200 miles (322 kilometers) an hour. Boats that go this fast are also very dangerous. Many drivers have been injured when their boats flipped over at high speeds.

HOVERCRAFT

The **hovercraft** (HUV er KRAFT) is a machine that can travel over land or water without wheels, wings, or floats. It hovers on air.

The hovercraft is also called an air-cushion vehicle. A large fan pushes air down from the bottom of the vehicle. A skirt around the bottom of the craft holds the air in and causes the craft to hover, or float.

Hovercraft are used by the military and by the public for transportation. The biggest hovercraft can carry 250 people and 30 automobiles.

Big airplane-like propellers power a hovercraft across land or water.

CRUISE SHIP

A cruise ship carries hundreds, even thousands, of passengers. Some ships are so big they may have movie theaters, bowling alleys, swimming pools, and even shopping malls on board.

A cruise ship is more like a floating city than a ship. They have all the comforts of home, except that a crew does all the work and prepares all the meals.

Cruise ships visit ports all over the world. Whether you enjoy traveling or just relaxing, a cruise ship is a great way to go.

Cruise ships are like floating hotels.

BATTLESHIP

One of the biggest ships in the U.S. Navy is the battleship. Picture three football fields end to end and you will have the size of a typical battleship.

Battleships are very powerful. They have huge guns and missiles that can destroy enemy ships and aircraft.

Battleship USS Wisconsin fires off one of her 16-inch guns during a training exercise.

Crew members stand on deck as their battleship gets under way.

The battleship itself is protected by **armored** (AHR murd) steel up to 16 inches (40.64 centimeters) thick.

Battleships usually travel as part of a carrier battle group. The carrier battle group may have one or more aircraft carriers led by battleships, cruisers, destroyers, and other ships.

FUN ON THE WATER

Riding personal watercraft is one way to enjoy the water. Personal watercraft machines use a jet of water, at the rear of the craft, to move riders along the water's surface.

Personal watercraft have handlebars like a bicycle. As the rider turns the handlebars the jet of water moves to steer the craft.

One kind of personal watercraft is designed for one rider. Standing or kneeling, a skilled rider can cruise at speeds over 40 miles an hour (64.4 kilometers). Riders enjoy jumping their machines over waves and making sharp turns.

A second style of personal watercraft allows the rider to sit. Some of these machines are big enough to hold three riders at once.

Personal watercraft riders can stand or kneel when jumping the waves.

GLOSSARY

armored (AHR murd) — having a protective covering

buoy (BOO ee) — a floating object anchored in water used to mark off an area

extreme (ik STREEM) — beyond normal limits as in extremely big or extremely powerful

hovercraft (HUV er KRAFT) — a motorized vehicle that floats on air a few feet above water or land

hydrofoil (HY druh FOYL) — a craft designed for action in or on the water

nuclear powered — (NOO klee ur POW erd) powered by the energy released when tiny bits, called atoms, are split

A skilled rider performs tricks on his extreme machine.

INDEX

FURTHER READING

Find out more about Extreme Machines with these helpful books:
Pelta, Kathy. *The U.S. Navy.* Lerner Publications Company, 1990.
Let's Discover Ships and Boats. Raintree Publishers, 1986.